I am a
Muslim

James Nixon

Photography by Chris Fairclough

W

FRANKLIN WATTS
LONDON•SYDNEY

First published in 2007 by
Franklin Watts
338 Euston Road
London NW1 3BH

Franklin Watts Australia
Level 17/207 Kent Street
Sydney NSW 2000

In this book we use the abbreviation (pbuh) for 'peace be upon him', a sign of respect for the Prophet Muhammad.

ISBN: 978 0 7496 7448 9 (hbk)
ISBN: 978 0 7496 7460 1 (pbk)

Dewey classification number: 297

A CIP catalogue record for this book is available from the British Library.

Planning and production by Discovery Books Limited
Editor: James Nixon
Designer: Ian Winton
Photography: Chris Fairclough
Series advisors: Diana Bentley MA and Dee Reid MA,
Fellows of Oxford Brookes University

The author, packager and publisher would like to thank the following
people for their participation in this book: Samiya and Sanya Latif and family;
Nottingham Islamia School and Bobbersmill Community Centre, Nottingham.

All photographs by Chris Fairclough.

Printed in China

Franklin Watts is a division of Hachette Children's books,
an Hachette Livre UK company.

Contents

I am a Muslim

My name is Samiya
and I am a Muslim.
My religion is Islam.

We believe in Allah
and his prophet,
Muhammad (pbuh).

5

Worshipping Allah

As Muslims we show our love for Allah.

We worship Allah together in a mosque.

Showing respect

Before we pray we we take off our shoes...

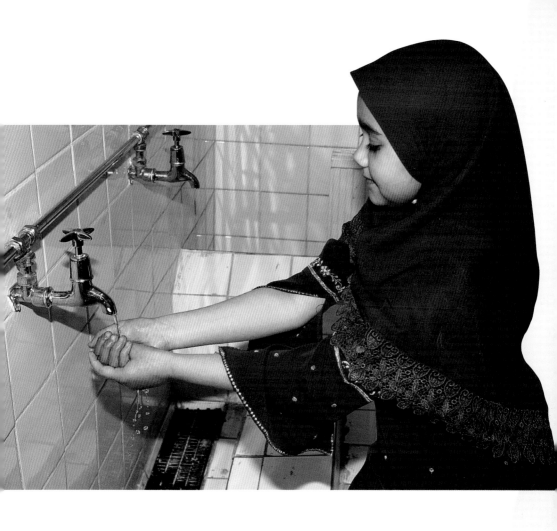

...and wash our
hands and face.

How we pray

Muslims pray to Allah five times a day.

We kneel on a mat
and bow to Allah.

The Qur'an

Our holy book is the Qur'an. We believe it is the word of Allah.

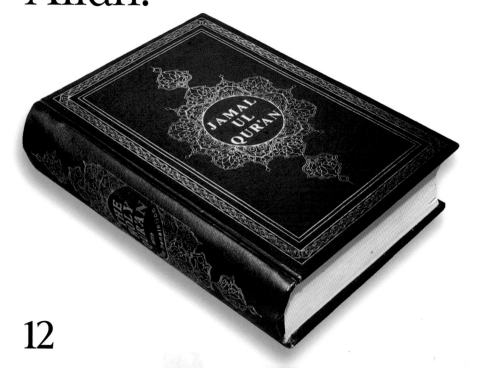

Muhammad (pbuh) wrote down Allah's words. It tells us how to live.

Learning the Qur'an

We respect the Qur'an. It must never touch the ground.

I learn parts
of it by heart.

Helping others

At the mosque we help raise money for the poor.

Sometimes I sell cakes.

Ramadan

During the month of Ramadan...

...adults do not eat or drink in the daytime.

They only eat after sunset.

Festivals

When Ramadan is over we have the festival of Eid.

I can wear my new
salwar kameez.

Allah is good

I like being a Muslim.

Allah
helps me
lead a
good life.

23

Word bank

Look back for these words and pictures.

Kneel

Money

Mosque

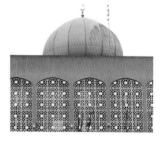

Muslim

Pray

Qur'an

Ramadan

Salwar kameez

Wash